Lilies
IN THE *Field*

KATHY
ANDERSON

 FriesenPress

Suite 300 - 990 Fort St
Victoria, BC, V8V 3K2
Canada

www.friesenpress.com

ISBN
978-1-5255-4372-2 (Hardcover)
978-1-5255-4373-9 (Paperback)
978-1-5255-4374-6 (eBook)

1. BIOGRAPHY & AUTOBIOGRAPHY, MILITARY

Distributed to the trade by The Ingram Book Company

To my family

TABLE OF CONTENTS

"Therefore I tell you, do not worry about your life and what you will eat, or about your body and what you will wear. For life is more than food and the body more than clothing.

Notice the ravens: they do not sow or reap; they have neither storehouse nor barn, yet God feeds them. How much more important are you than birds!

Can any of you by worrying add a moment to your life-span? If even the smallest things are beyond your control, why are you anxious about the rest?

Notice how the lilies of the field grow. They do not toil or spin. But I tell you, not even Solomon in all his splendor was dressed like one of them."

Luke 12:22–27

Lord, make me an instrument of your peace:
where there is hatred, let me sow love;
where there is injury, pardon;
where there is doubt, faith;
where there is despair, hope;
where there is darkness, light;
where there is sadness, joy.

O divine Master, grant that I may not so much seek
to be consoled as to console,
to be understood as to understand,
to be loved as to love.
For it is in giving that we receive,
it is in pardoning that we are pardoned,
and it is in dying that we are born to eternal life.
Amen.

Prayer of St. Francis of Assisi

Introduction
Nuclear War

*I*t was the summer of 2006. I was in Cambridge, Massachusetts, for an internship at MIT. I was working late. Looking at me in that moment, you might have thought I was on top of the world. I was twenty-seven years old. I had just finished the first year of my PhD program in computer science at the University of Notre Dame, and I was about to start an internship at MIT that I had long dreamed of. I had earned a master's degree in computer science from the University of Massachusetts, Amherst, and a bachelor's degree in math from Villanova University. A child of a military officer, I had also pursued a military career in the Air Force, just like my mom.

Academically, I was advancing, going as far as I could go. I had wanted to become a scientist so badly while serving in the Air Force. Now those dreams were finally coming true after a successful military career that had taken me to California, Montana, and Indiana. I had earned a scholarship through ROTC, made it through boot camp, and completed all my military training. As an officer, I served as a deputy flight commander and a missile combat crew commander, achieving the rank of captain. I earned my master's degree while working full-time in the Air Force. I had already seen so much of the world. On top of that, I had a wonderful family, my parents and two brothers, who were loving, supportive, and generous. By all accounts, my life seemed full of meaning, purpose, and the pursuit of my dreams.

I arrived in Cambridge on June 1, 2006. By June 23, I was in the hospital. By that Christmas, I was suicidal.

This book is my story. In telling it, I pull together pieces from my childhood, adolescence, college years, and my first psychotic break in 2006. There's no single reason that can explain what happened or everything else that happened after that first hospitalization. There is no primary cause—no simple way to understand my journey through a long battle with mental illness to understand where I am today. During this time, I didn't always understand what was happening to me. I didn't always see a plan or purpose in my experiences. But today as I look back, I see important lessons to share. I have experienced things that I never thought would happen to me. Somehow, everything I went through has given me wisdom, and I have grown and changed. I have also remained myself.

When I think back to that summer in Cambridge, I remember that the trip from South Bend, Indiana, to Massachusetts was lonely and exhausting. Like so many military children and officers, I had never lived in the same place for more than a few years. I didn't know anyone at MIT. I was away from my family, and I was beyond tired. My exhaustion had begun two years earlier, when I worked night shifts as a missile combat crew commander. I had grown incredibly sleep deprived from those years of duty. My sleeplessness continued through my first year at Notre Dame.

But my story, like all of my stories, began even before that. Since college, I had battled serious physical ailments. I suffered from long-untreated internal-health issues. My mind and body were long worn down by the time I arrived at MIT. I experienced years of unexplained symptoms: weakness, fatigue, pain, and photophobia (pain in the eyes due to light exposure). I worked through all the physical pain and even surgery. I did not always receive the treatment I needed. The physical and mental battles grew exhausting and frustrating.

My mental and physical health journeys are intertwined with my spiritual journey. Sometimes it has been a battle, sometimes a source of great joy, and sometimes despair. Spiritually, I have asked many questions and found many answers. I have wrestled with doubts, I have lost faith, searched to regain it, and looked in unusual places. These are the three journeys of my life. They each happened in their own time, and they all came together. They define me. From all my journeys, I gained a new depth of understanding about myself, my family, and the world around me. Any one of these journeys would have been enough for a lifetime of experiences, but I wouldn't be who I am today without having been through them all.

One night, I was working late in the lab at MIT, and the world around me suddenly changed. I became convinced that everyone was out to get me. A coworker invited me to look at an image of the solar system that was part of his research. "Look at this screen," he said. My eyes fell on an image of the planets orbiting the sun. Suddenly, that image got lodged in my head, and a panic set in that would not let me go. I was seized by fear that the government was trying to hypnotize me through that image. They were trying to take control of my mind.

When you have a psychotic break, your brain can't tell what's normal and what's delusional. Everything seems real, and everything fits together like a perfect puzzle. Once the delusion sets in, everything you see feeds it and confirms it. Every person or object is just more evidence that the delusion must be real. There is no way for your brain to do a reality check. I don't know if it was the image on the screen in particular, or if I simply saw it at the moment of my breakdown, but from that moment on, I lived in fear of everything around me.

I wandered around the lab and thought the Virgin Mary was talking to me from a whiteboard. I believed I was about to be crucified like Jesus, that I would die and go to heaven and never see my family again.

At some point I walked to the library down the block from the lab. I saw a figure in white that terrified me. I believed it was a ghost. Even the street signs were glowing with messages.

As I drove home, I followed signs toward Providence and New Jerusalem, even though they took me away from my apartment. The entire world was alive with signs for me, and they were all connected. In my mind, all these sights and signs were real, even though I could not explain them. My fear was deep, but so was my certainty that everything I saw or feared was actually happening. My imagination was torturing me.

Later that same night, back in my apartment, I heard missiles flying outside my window. I was convinced a war had begun—that we were in the midst of a nuclear conflict and a great spiritual battle. I saw gates opening in the heavens. I thought all the dead people were coming from hell into heaven. I had given my life to God, and now it was really happening. I did not question these events, the sights, or the sounds.

That night, unable to sleep, I called my mom. We talked throughout the night. I told her everything. She listened from her home in Maryland, trying to talk me down and keep me calm, but her denials of my delusions only strengthened my convictions that the devil was outside my door and that I was going to have a child through God like the Virgin Mary.

At some point, my mom told me that my dad was getting on the next flight to Massachusetts to be with me. I don't remember when he arrived or how long he stayed, only that he tried to get me to rest with sleep aids, and they didn't work. Soon enough, my delusions and paranoia landed on him. One moment, I believed my dad, whose name is Joseph, was the father of Jesus. The next moment, I believed he was the devil, who had gotten inside my apartment. Though I was probably misplacing ordinary items in my delusional state, I believed my religious relics were disappearing from my apartment as well.

Somehow in the midst of all this, I remembered that the School Sisters of Notre Dame, a religious order that I had once thought about joining, advised me to see the chaplain on Hamscom Air Force Base, just outside of Boston. Deathly afraid of my dad, I drove to the chaplain's office, hoping I had escaped the devil. My dad had no idea where I had gone. I felt safe with the chaplain and went to the Department of Veterans Affairs (VA) hospital on his advice.

I stayed in the Boston VA hospital for ten or twelve days. The experience is a blur of locked doors, strange people, and medications. The chaplain's office contacted my parents, who were listed as my emergency contacts.

My mind cleared a little while in the hospital, but I was afraid of being locked in, still not entirely sure of where I was. Eventually, I checked myself out, against medical advice. Years later in my string of hospitalizations, my parents obtained a court order to prevent me from checking out of the hospital on my own. That time, however, I could walk out, even though I was not well.

Just after I was released, I noticed that my hair seemed longer. I felt like Jesus's sister. In my mind, I *was* Jesus's sister. My delusions were as strong as ever.

One day during that period, I was driving with my dad, and we stopped near a bridge for something to eat. I thought the bridge was the gateway to heaven and that I could cross over it to live with God, to die, just like Jesus. However, I chose not to go, to remain on Earth instead.

This was my first psychotic break and hospitalization. Dozens more followed over the next seven years. It grew to the point where I no longer wanted to live. I became so hopeless and depressed at my condition that I just wanted to end it. But there is a difference between wanting to die and not wanting to live in fear and pain anymore.

The rest of my journey involved more wrestling, more unexpected turns through schizoaffective disorder, my body's journey through deterioration, and my spiritual journey away from and back to God. The end of my story is not yet written. I want to take you through the struggle and the joy, to see how a vocation can be sought and found and how far a soul can travel.

Chapter 1
Child of God

I was born on October 4, 1978, in the Netherlands. I don't remember much about the place of my birth, where I lived with my parents and older brother, Patrick, until I was four. However, I do know that living in Europe was the happiest time of my life. My childhood, where my story begins, was idyllic.

In the Netherlands, we lived in a rented three-story triplex. Our suburban neighborhood was filled with neighbors like Mr. von Fleet, who gave Patrick and me chocolates when we came over to visit.

I know from my mother's stories that I was an imaginative child. I once hid under a tent while my mom kissed a doll in my bed goodnight. I was thrilled that I had tricked her into believing the doll was me. Another time, around age three, I accidently locked myself in my room and was convinced I would have to eat food slipped on a tray under my door forever. Eventually, my parents calmed me down, and helped me free myself from my room. Then they took away the keys to the doors.

I was also a talkative child. One day while sitting with my mom on a bus, I leaned over to the passenger in the seat ahead of us and declared that I had gone to the bathroom all by myself. My mom was deeply embarrassed but thought the person was probably Dutch and didn't understand my humiliating statement. But as my mom and I got up to leave, the passenger turned to us and said, "Goodbye," in perfect English. He had understood everything. My mother was duly embarrassed.

I also remember the arrival of a new sibling. I was just beginning to understand my mom's pregnancy, and I held her hand and asked, "What's his name going to be again?" She answered, "Peter." When my little brother was born in 1983, our family of five was complete.

My mom, who was born in Harrisburg, Pennsylvania, was stationed with the Air Force at Camp New Amsterdam, the Netherlands. She was born on November 6, 1946, in Harrisburg, PA. My dad was a civil servant with the Defense Commissary Agency (DeCA). He was born on March 19, 1942, in Dade City, Fl.

My dad's family descended from German immigrants. My mom's family immigrated to the US from Italy on my grandfather's side and Lithuania on my grandmother's side.

My mom is a great storyteller. Her childhood was filled with funny adventures, much like my own. Once she gave her brother pills that she said would make him fly, and he leaped off the bed to see if they would work. Another time, while in a full leg cast, my mom dragged an old Christmas tree up from the basement and covered it in a sheet, tucking the "ghost" into my grandmother's closet to frighten her on Halloween. She delighted in my grandmother's scream the next morning when my grandmother opened the closet and the "ghost" fell out. No one in the family believed my mother could have done all that while in a leg cast. My mom also once laid a stray cat in her sister's playpen as a gift for her sister (to her mother's chagrin), and once she accidently bloodied her brother's nose while they were trying out his new boxing gloves.

When I was four, my mom got a new assignment, and we moved to Ramstein Air Base in Germany. I have much more vivid memories of Germany than I do of the Netherlands. In the city of Mackenbach, our house was one story with a basement. Our neighbors were German and American. We were surrounded by other service families, who were sprinkled around the German neighborhood.

We lived near the base, and my dad was busy working too. He managed a warehouse for the Sembach Air Base commissary and won several awards, receiving lots of recognition for his work on the base. My mom and dad always shared the household responsibilities. I also always admired my dad for following my mom and her career in the Air Force for twenty years. I admired how he shared in all the cooking, did the laundry, and took care of us kids equally.

~

As a child, I looked for God in church. I wish I could remember our church in the Netherlands. Our church in Germany was simple, small, and open. It was a pentagon-shaped building on the base that was shared by all denominations. The building was simple without the usual stained glass or crucifix or stations of the cross, because other denominations don't use Catholic icons. Mass was simple too without putting on airs. I was closest to God during that time in Germany. I prayed a lot. I tried to see Jesus in everyone. Years later, I joined the Air Force to find God again.

Our family went to Mass every weekend for the Saturday evening vigil. Our lives were tied to the church. We practiced our faith regularly; it was a steady part of our lives. Patrick and I both became altar servers.

It was around this time that Pope John Paul II addressed the question of whether girls should be allowed to serve along with boys. The pope eventually decided to allow bishops and priests to make the final choice. Even though all girls were technically allowed to serve, every bishop or priest still had the power to prevent girls from being altar servers. I loved being an altar server, and I would have been heartbroken if I couldn't do it anymore. Luckily, I didn't have to face that choice. I remember our priest reassuring my mother, "The Pope isn't coming to Ramstein." He was something of a pioneer for girls in the church, perhaps without even knowing it.

I loved everything about church and God. You could say that I loved God to death and felt most close to God at those base masses. God was my best friend. I loved to sing the fast-paced songs. I remember the music vividly. Outside of Germany, I found church music dull and slow, nothing like what I'd heard when I was a child.

Because no religious schools were available for us on base, we went the base public school. This meant we attended CCD, which stands for Confraternity of Christian

Doctrine. These are classes for religious education that Catholic children take when they can't go to a Catholic school. In CCD, I learned about loving Jesus, being kind to neighbors, and seeing the image of God in everyone. We also prepared for our sacraments.

My parents were just as devout. They helped with the parish council. My parents truly set the example for us with their faith. They both were lifelong Catholics. My dad was a deacon at one point. My mom continues to be deeply charitable to anyone in need.

~

The other big part of my life was the military. My mom tells me that I used to dream of serving the church and becoming an Air Force pilot. Our life was our neighborhood and the base, which consisted of thirty to forty buildings. On base and in our community, the military was part of the wider culture, and there was a lot of cultural exchange. I was no stranger to diversity, seeing interracial marriages, and having friends of all backgrounds. Only when we moved to the US did I realize how separately people lived. In the US, I saw for the first time how race was a heated issue that divided people. In Europe, I remained sheltered from such division.

My time in Germany was the happiest of my life. I was as close to God as I have ever been. Life was church, school, and the love of my family. We visited different castles every Sunday. We rode our bikes and ate in German restaurants. I played with GI Joes and booby-trapped the house with Patrick. He and I also joined scout troops. One time,

Patrick's scout troop rode their bicycles all the way to the border of the former state of Czechoslovakia. In the girl scouts, we camped outside the base, and I wished the girls could do more adventurous things, like the boys. My family attended car shows, set off fireworks on holidays, and we kids climbed trees in our backyard. My school even went on class ski trips to Austria. We were free and happy and very lucky. We also had mischievous adventures like blowing up our GI Joes with leftover fireworks or jumping out of our bedroom windows. Mostly we attended school on base with American teachers and studied German once a week. I also learned to crochet and to play the flute.

Our life included regular travel. Every year on our vacation, my family visited a new European country. Additionally, every summer, Patrick and I spent five weeks with relatives in the US: three weeks with one aunt in Florida and two weeks with another aunt in Pennsylvania. In Germany, we didn't have American radio, and the only television was the Armed Forces Network. The base had one movie theater. We rarely went to the movies though, and the movies came out six to eight months after people in the States had seen them.

During those summers with my relatives in the US, I learned a lot about American culture that I didn't know in Germany. I watched endless movies and cartoons that my aunt recorded on VHS tapes for us during the school year. I marveled at the number of TV channels *and* commercials. All summer, we swam with our cousins in their pool and played at water parks.

I hated being the middle child. I got blamed for a lot of the trouble that my two brothers started. But we were still a team, and we made our own trouble together. When we traveled around Europe with our visiting aunts and uncles, Patrick would lead the way into mischief, and I would follow. Once when we were traveling in Berchtesgaden, Germany, we snuck up to a pair of slot machines and started playing. I had two dollars' worth of quarters, and I started pulling on the machines. I actually won twenty dollars, but Patrick tattled, and I got in trouble. Another time in Italy, I followed Patrick to play in the Trevi Fountain, but a police officer pulled us out and escorted us back to our embarrassed parents.

After twenty years of being in the service, my mom retired from the Air Force, and we moved from Germany. I don't remember being told that we would leave Germany. I also don't remember packing up our home, saying goodbye to my friends, or the long plane ride across the ocean. I don't remember wondering what my new life would be like or feeling like I would miss my life in Germany. It was 1990, and I was eleven years old, about to enter seventh grade.

We had lived in Germany for seven years, and we had lived in Europe for my entire life. Now we were going "home" to the United States. Europe was all that I had known. It was my entire life. I knew we were Americans, but I had never lived in the States for longer than five weeks each summer. I wasn't afraid of the move, and I wasn't unwilling to go to a new home. I was a brave child, and I wasn't anxious about my future. I just put one foot in front of the other and kept walking.

The things I knew back then were that I loved God and that my soul was the part of the life that God gave me when I was born. I knew God was part of my being, and that he knew the deepest desires of my soul. I was joyful in this relationship with God. My joy was bigger than happiness. Happiness is a superficial feeling. What I had was joy, an everlasting peace.

Chapter 2
American Dream

*W*hen we finally arrived in America from Germany, my family went in three directions. My parents and Peter went to Bolling Air Force Base to get our new life situated and to find us a home. My mom also needed to sort out her retirement from the Air Force, and my dad needed to get his job situation arranged. Patrick went to stay with my aunt and uncle in Florida. I went to Middletown, Pennsylvania, to live with my mom's sister, Aunt Lin, her husband, Uncle Greg, and my cousins, Carolyn and Laura, who were around five and two years old. For the next two and a half months, I lived in a new family of girls in a lovely suburban neighborhood, missing my brothers and my parents especially. My aunt's home was a one-story house that my grandad built. I had my own bedroom, which I liked. Though I missed my parents, the idea of being separated from them did not alarm me. We had visited these relatives every summer for several years. Going there felt like I was just going for an extended summer stay.

I can't imagine what my parents' adjustment was like. They had been living outside the continental US for over thirteen years. Now they had to find a home for their three children and build a new life for all of us.

My aunt and uncle took me to Mass regularly. I was no longer an altar server, like I was in Germany, and I missed participating in the Mass. Altar service was not the only way I had participated in the liturgy. I also liked to sing. The music in Germany had been lively, fast, and fun to sing along to. I had grown used to finding God with my voice and singing along with everyone around me. Masses in Middletown were quite different. The homilies were long, and the music was slow. The singing was mostly done by the choir without participation from the rest of us. We were like their audience—like spectators instead of participants. Mass became about watching and listening instead of *doing*. And these American songs were like operas: difficult and formal. The familiar music was gone, and so were the simple surroundings of the Ramstein base church, replaced with a church that was enormous and ornately decorated. Statues, icons, stained glass, stations of the cross, and saints surrounded me. The look and feel of this, and many other American churches I attended throughout my life, were everything my beloved church in Germany was not.

At the time, at age eleven, I wondered where God was. I had always been able to find God during Mass, in its simplicity and beauty. Now I no longer enjoyed Mass like I once did. I had lost my idyllic childhood life in Europe, and I felt that I was losing God too. I wondered if I could ever find God again in those new surroundings. I was not yet filled with the sense that I had lost God as my best friend and constant source of comfort. That loss came later, after I reunited with my parents and brothers. For the moment, life in the United States was a series of adjustments.

I was deeply accustomed to military base life, which involved a constant rotation of people in and out of my life. Friends on the base would come and go. People moved in and out all the time. Change was a normal part of life, and I was used to seeing people one day and missing them the next. This kind of exposure to change while living in Germany may have prepared me well for moving to America. I was not frightened by changes in location or surroundings. I adjusted well to Pennsylvania while I waited for my parents to return for me.

Despite all the changes of base life, my parents had been a steady and reliable presence in Germany. My mom had plenty of vacation days in the Air Force, and we did a lot of things together. Now my parents were not living with me for the first time in my life. I knew they were planning to have us all back together soon and that I would not be separated from them forever, but I still missed them. We talked on the phone often.

I did not experience the kind of culture shock you might imagine when moving to a different country. At Ramstein, though we were living in Germany, our life was very American. We shopped at the base commissary. We ate American food. We spoke English. We were educated with other Americans. We were like a little island of Americans surrounded by German culture. So, when I moved back to the US, I did not undergo a radical adjustment. I did not have to learn a new language or adapt to a foreign culture. In many ways, our move from Germany was not so different from moving from one state to another.

However, one big shock I did experience was living outside the military culture for the first time. On a military base, respect and good behavior are expected. I was surrounded by officers who were used to order, discipline, and respecting rank. Kids respected their elders, obeyed their teachers, and treated each other kindly. We did not tease or bully anybody. Everyone was from somewhere else, so we were used to seeing and accepting differences. The constant flow of strangers meant we made friends easily. In the US, it quickly became clear that shifting away from military culture opened the door to a different reality: a new and sudden lack of respect for others. Rules and expectations for how to treat others were lax or even nonexistent. Teasing, bullying, disrespect, and disobedience were all "normal" and tolerated far beyond what would have been allowed back on the base.

As American as I felt, living on a foreign base still made us different from our peers, who grew up in typical American cities. One difference was my lack of exposure to pop culture. In Germany, as I mentioned, we only had the Armed Forces Network TV channel and no American radio. So, my childhood world did not center on knowing current movie stars, listening to hit music, or being up on the latest trends. For clothes, we had shopped mostly on base, with limited selection. Back then our concern wasn't having the coolest jeans or trendiest clothes. We were just kids who wanted to play and enjoy life. So, I arrived in the States not knowing what most other kids knew about television, radio, movies, and fashion.

I started seventh grade at a Catholic school in Pennsylvania, but by October, my parents had found us a home in Maryland. We could finally live together again as a family. Our new home was only three hours south of my aunt and uncle in Pennsylvania.

I don't remember the drive from Middletown to Waldorf, whether it passed quickly or slowly. It was uneventful, much like the flight from Germany. I don't remember being nervous or afraid. As a family, we were all taking this next step together. We moved forward without looking back. I can picture my brothers and me in the back seat while my parents navigated us toward our new life.

Though the particulars of that day are hazy, the drive to Maryland marked the end of my transition to living in the US. I was no longer waiting for my parents to bring me to our new life; I was actually on my way. We were no longer an American family living on foreign soil on a military base. We were no longer the military kids who moved around with my mom's career and lived in many different places. We would not travel through European countries during my mom's vacation days anymore. Our new normal would be Maryland until I graduated from high school and went to college. I would live in one place for the rest of my childhood.

From Waldorf, I would drive with my mom back to visit Aunt Lin and Uncle Greg regularly. After their third daughter, Rachel, was born, I would babysit all three of my cousins during our visits. On those drives, my mom would tell me stories about her childhood. My first home in Pennsylvania became a warm place to visit, and my mom and her sister kept our families close in touch.

~

They say it takes a village to raise a child, and we certainly had wonderful neighbors in our new Waldorf neighborhood. Our little village was a tight, caring set of Air Force families who could understand our experiences and our lives. There were many other kids for us to play with and develop close friendships with. My little brother, Peter, found his best friend, Zach, on our block. Zach's family embraced Peter like one of their own and treated him like another son.

I found my own best friends as well. One had a father who also had been in the Air Force and was an Air Force One pilot for the president. Our next-door neighbors were especially dear to me. I babysat their kids and played with their oldest and middle children. I also babysat for many other families in our neighborhood to earn extra cash. In the morning before school, I would walk with Ms. Pam, our next-door neighbor. I was enamored with Mr. Pam's son, Chris, who I thought was cute. I played soccer and made more friends on my team, some of whom went to the same high school as me. My dad also built us a wooden treehouse in our backyard.

In many ways, our new life in Waldorf was wonderful, almost as idyllic as life back in Europe. We were surrounded by loving families and a stable group of friends. Our neighborhood had a close family feel. I didn't have to think about moving again or losing friends constantly because of military reassignments. While living away from an Air Force base was new to me, our steady little life had its advantages.

Both of my parents continued to work when we were in Maryland, even though my mom had retired from the Air Force. My dad worked at DeCA headquarters in Virginia for the next fifteen years, dutifully commuting two hours each way every single day. He made a huge sacrifice for our family, just as he always had, and worked extremely hard. My mom drove an hour to work each way as well. I knew my parents were making big sacrifices for us to have a good life. I thought about that when I missed them and was unable to see them until late most nights. Back in Germany, we stayed with babysitters while our parents worked, but now Patrick and I were old enough to look after ourselves and Peter.

Sometime in the late 1990s, many of our old and beloved neighbors moved away. Once again, I said goodbye to my friends. Living in a neighborhood did not shield me from losing friends like I had on base. After our dearest neighbors moved away, our once-close neighborhood no longer had the same sense of family or community bonds. We no longer held block parties on the court. Our new neighbors weren't as interested in getting to know us or each other. Our little neighborhood crew thinned out, but my family kept moving forward.

I finished seventh grade at Matthew Henson Middle School, a public school near Waldorf. Being at a public school was a big change for me, coming first from school on base and then from a Catholic school in Middletown. Most of the kids in my new school had never traveled outside of the US. They were not used to seeing people of different cultures or the kind of diversity that was normal on a military base. I was so accustomed to a mix of backgrounds, never thinking people who were different from me were strange or anything to be afraid of. Now I know how lucky I was to have such an upbringing. To be exposed to diversity, to embrace difference, was a gift.

I learned this by being the one who was different in seventh grade. I discovered how unfriendly children could be to people who are different in some way. I was called "Swiss Mountain Girl," "ho," and many other even harsher names. Though I thought my clothes were nice, they were not in the latest style or trend, so I stuck out even more. I looked and acted differently from everyone else. I had no idea who the hottest TV stars were, what movies were cool, or what music was popular. The other kids talked about things that I didn't know about. I also didn't behave the way they did: ignoring the teachers, throwing paper across the room during class, disrespecting each other, and saying nasty things. Throughout all the taunting, I never wanted to fight back because I couldn't imagine hurting anyone. Being new, somewhat foreign, and just plain different made me an easy target for teasing, cruelty, and exclusion. Sometimes I would cry when my dad picked me up from school.

All this time, I tried to pray for those kids. I might not have known where God was, but I still could pray for my enemies and hope they would change. Nonetheless, it was hard to be the new girl, the one everyone was leaving out and picking on.

Despite how hard that time was for me, I would not trade growing up in the military for anything. My childhood in the Netherlands and Germany introduced me to different cultures and set my dreams in motion. I went on to have my own military career, and I never stopped looking for God or for the good in other people.

After my terrible seventh-grade year, my parents put me in St. Peter's Middle School and later St. Mary's Ryken High School. Transferring to a Catholic school was a huge relief. I took religion classes every day. For the first time in a long time, I felt reconnected to God. I also befriended another new girl who no one wanted to hang out with. We walked together and tried to be kind to each other and to do what Jesus would do.

In some ways, my quest for God had brought me all the way there, to that Catholic middle school, where I might find some relief from my peers and continue seeking God. I had lost God for a while, but I was starting to find him again, away from the bullying. I felt myself drawing closer to God in my new school. This remained a theme for my entire life—looking for God in different places. I saw glimpses, but I always wanted to be closer. I continued searching throughout high school, at Catholic college, and then in the Air Force—my quest seemingly unending, my search never over.

Chapter 3
Family History

The bullying I experienced at my first middle school led to a mild depression. I did not understand why I was targeted for cruelty, and I saw no way out of my daily existence of teasing, taunting, and being left out. At such a young age, when friendships are crucial to one's developing sense of self, it was hard to cope with such treatment without feeling depressed. There were no national campaigns against bullying back then, no awareness or training for parents and teachers. Unlike today, kids were not educated about the dangers and effects of bullying. I was fortunate that my parents moved me away from the toxic environment of my first Maryland middle school and placed me into a new school. After I changed schools, my life improved, and my depression lifted. However, my younger brother, Peter, was not so lucky.

He was also being teased and bullied. Like me, he was a quiet kid. I think I had a vague sense of what was happening, but my family rarely talked about bullying. Peter stayed quiet about how he was treated at school. I imagine it was painful and embarrassing for him to be bullied and excluded. Peter, in general, kept to himself, so I didn't know the extent of his suffering at school. Now I know that the bullying stuck with him for a long time, that those kids had been very cruel to him, and that it had a serious effect on him. He did, however, have a close-knit circle of friends who always came to his defense.

Sometime after I joined the Air Force, I learned from my parents that Peter had been hospitalized. By then he was in high school. My parents told me on the phone that Peter had exploded with rage and despair during a routine doctor's visit. He finally let on about the bullying. This was the first time my parents really learned about what was happening and how deeply it had affected Peter. To their credit, they got him into counseling right away, after he was released from the hospital. I didn't know the details of Peter's hospitalization. I knew he was in a psychiatric ward, like the one I found myself in many years later in Massachusetts. The parallel sticks with me: both Peter and me in the hospital, wrestling with our mental health.

I can't say for sure what I or anyone else noticed when we were kids. Peter was just my baby brother. You never imagine your younger sibling dealing with such a major issue, especially in high school when he was still growing into the person he would become. Later on, Peter dealt with obsessive compulsive disorder (OCD) and generalized anxiety disorder. I also struggle with anxiety, for which I take medication.

Looking deeper into my family history, it's clear that anxiety begins with my dad. Maybe it begins even further back than him. My dad has always been a worrier. He used to fret about starting up the grill. He feared it would explode and destroy the house. The funny thing is, I worried right alongside him. I remember asking him once, while he fired up the grill for dinner, how he knew it wasn't going to explode. He said he didn't know for sure but that he truly thought it *could* explode. Sometimes our worries fueled each other in this way.

Today my dad still worries about many things, big and small. He worries himself sick sometimes about things that *might* or might not be true. He thinks of the worst-case scenario. The highly improbable disastrous outcome is always on his mind. I know my dad also worried himself sick over Peter and me. Now that he's retired, his worrying has increased. He doesn't take anxiety medication or get professional help. In some ways, his anxiety falls within the realm of normal worry. In other ways, it distracts him from his daily life and causes him unnecessary stress.

I can look to my mom for clues about our family's mental health too. Sometimes her tendency toward perfectionism looks like OCD. She'll get engrossed in a task or obsessed with finding a missing item. Sometimes she'll spend several hours trying to wrap a present perfectly, precisely measuring and drawing lines on the paper. Or she'll hunt for a lost file for half a day until she finds it.

After I was hospitalized for the first time in Massachusetts, I went home to stay with my parents for a while. I was upset because I thought my Air Force career was over. Then my mom shared something with me that I will never forget. I don't remember her exact words. I was heavily medicated and still somewhat confused about my surroundings. I wasn't exactly thinking clearly at the moment, and I know I didn't process the information until much later. However, I do remember that at one point she sat on my bed and told me that she, too, had once experienced a psychotic break and been hospitalized.

Back then, when she was in her twenties, such a thing was shameful to admit. It was taboo to talk about, let alone seek help for it. My mother had never shared this with me before. She chose to share that part of her story with me while I was in my own deep crisis to show me that she understood exactly what I was going through, and that I would recover from my psychotic break too. My mom's break was caused by stress and fatigue from the Air Force, just like mine, in addition to her disappointment at not getting into medical school. She had also worked overnight shifts that led to insomnia and sleep deprivation, and she had worked in a high-pressure environment for a long time. The strain eventually became too much. These were all things that we shared in common. My mom was put on medication for about a year and saw a doctor regularly. I think everyone thought that would be part of my story too—that after a year I would recover. However, my recovery took much longer than hers. I had many more episodes than my mother ever had, and my fight to regain health and stability lasted many more years.

My mom's experiences helped me get through my own psychotic break. In fact, the experience brought us closer, though I had always been close to my parents. While I was in the Air Force, I relied on my mom and dad for support.

When I had my first psychotic break, my parents were there for me. They dropped everything and came out to help me.

Today I visit them at Christmas, and they visit me in late spring. My parents still live in Maryland. We are active together. We are not ones to sit around. We clean the house and run errands together. But my mom and dad are in their seventies now, so I help around the house more when I'm home. My parents also visit me in South Bend when the weather is warm. Recently, I went with my parents to a Garth Brooks concert in South Bend, so you can see how active and loving they still are.

Patrick is the only member of my family who has not struggled with mental-health issues. Today we have a pleasant, cordial relationship. He is married with two wonderful sons. I wish I could be the kind of aunt to them that my parents' siblings were to me. They took me overnight and on trips. They also took me in for three months and became my second family. However, my mental illness has hindered me.

Today my mental illness is being carefully managed. I see my doctors and take my medication. I keep busy with classes and volunteer work. Sometimes it's frustrating to live with a mental illness because of the way people stigmatize me. They think I'm a danger or that I'm unpredictable or have nothing to offer. Mental illness can be frightening, and I have certainly experienced my own brain torturing me. But ever since I was a young girl, I have been a seeker. I have sought God, outlets for my spiritual fire, ways to serve others, and a vocation that I am passionate about. I know for certain that a vocation exists for every human being, even if he or she is delusional. God was still there with me during my episodes, just as God was with me before my psychotic break, and just as God is with me today.

Mental illness has often left me feeling frustrated and helpless, because I was unable to give what I knew I had inside to offer. Today I know what I'm capable of and what I have to give. I'm not a danger to anyone. I have much to give and much to offer to my family and the world. I am safe, reliable, and loving.

It has been a long road to get here, and it was only beginning for me in middle school. When I went to high school, life got busier. I look back on the person I was in high school, busy and active, surrounded by friends, playing sports, holding down jobs, and working steadily toward a military career and adult independence. I saw myself as full of potential, hope, and promise. Much of that promise was fulfilled for me, though my path was full of challenges— some of them devastating. It was also a path of deeper seeking, a cycle of drawing closer and then away from God. As I entered my high school and college years, a period of more searching and more frustration awaited me.

Chapter 4
Seeds of Doubt

*H*igh school passed quickly, each day beginning and ending with an hour-long bus ride with my friends. I loved the challenges of academics and extracurricular events. I was, and always have been, busy and involved in lots of activities. I hate to sit still, and I grow bored easily. I played flute and clarinet in the high-school band and joined the soccer and softball teams. In senior year, I joined the powerlifting team and won a national championship.

I had my eyes on the future and knew I had to set myself up for success. I got my first summer job when I was sixteen with the Department of the Army at Ft. Belvoir, Virginia. My parents bought me a used car, so I could make the forty-five-minute drive from home. I worked as an office automation clerk, filing papers and organizing contracts. The next year, I switched to the Department of the Air Force. Throughout college, I worked every summer under the Secretary of the Air Force for the Air Force Review Boards Agency, which reviews cases of service members who have been discharged with a less than "honorable" status. I even started saving when I was seventeen. My summer earnings were enough to invest in the stock market. Beginning with about seven stocks, I built a portfolio that went on to be worth over $13,000. Personal finance became my new hobby, partly because I was in love with math. I had discovered math back in middle school, especially algebra and logic puzzles.

While I was in high school, Patrick went off to Gannon University in Erie, Pennsylvania, leaving Peter and me to spend time together with our parents and friends. Our town of Waldorf was never quite the same after our first neighbors moved away. The closeness of our neighborhood had gone with them and never really returned. Trees were cleared for more and more new homes without really having the infrastructure to support all the expansion and growth. Today the roads are so crowded that it takes a long time to go anywhere, especially on weekends and holidays. I missed our old neighbors, and I also missed our lives in the Air Force in Germany. I associated that period of our lives with a great deal of happiness. Living on base within Air Force culture and really feeling like a child of God were things I wanted to recapture. Though I was serving in many ministries that kept me busy and made me happy, I still felt a spiritual longing for God. Nothing compared to my spiritual life in Germany or to the closeness I felt with God as a child. For a long time and in many different places, I tried to find that joy again.

My path always seemed to point toward the Air Force. In my senior year of high school, I applied to the Air Force Academy with intentions of becoming a pilot. I had excellent grades and recommendations. However, despite all my sports activities, I wasn't a great athlete. Determined to change that, I hired a personal trainer and began preparing for the academy's physical fitness test. I needed to train for pushups, a sixty-second sprint, and one complete pullup.

When the day of the fitness test finally arrived, I slipped, quite literally, all over the slick gym floor and missed the cutoff time for my sprint. I also discovered later that I was several inches too short to become a pilot. There was a shortage of candidates qualified to become pilots that year, and subsequently, I didn't get accepted to the Air Force Academy. I was deeply disappointed and upset, but looking back now, I realize it was one of the greatest blessings of my life. I came to learn that a career as a pilot would have involved living and dying by a checklist, ingrained routines, and attention to the smallest details. It definitely would not have been the kind of work that I could thrive on with my personality and desire for constant learning and new adventures.

I had been sure about my destiny to go to the Air Force Academy, but luckily, I had a backup plan. My application for an Air Force ROTC scholarship was accepted, and I was on my way to Villanova University near Philadelphia. I had never heard of Villanova. My mom told me about it because my Uncle Greg had gone there, and she encouraged me to apply. An ROTC scholarship supplemented with a university scholarship meant that, after my freshman year, I would have my education paid for.

During my first year at Villanova, I lived in a dorm on the south side of campus, complete with bunk beds, two roommates, communal bathrooms, a dining hall, and hours spent at local coffee shops. I majored in math, still loving the many aspects of its beauty. My interest expanded to computer science, and my fascination turned to using computers to solve math problems.

During college, I kept as busy as ever. When I came home on summer breaks, I played cards and built puzzles with my neighbor, Ms. Pam, and her family. I kept my summer job at the Air Force Review Boards Agency, even doing a magic trick at their board meetings every week. During the school year, I participated in the ROTC color guard/drill team. One year, we presented the colors at the opening ceremony for the Special Olympics. Another year, we were invited to present the colors during a Philadelphia Eagles football game. I also participated in German club.

On Fridays, everyone in Air Force ROTC met for leadership laboratory. Since the number of Air Force ROTC cadets was only about seven or eight, we met at St. Joseph University in Philadelphia, along with cadets from about sixteen other colleges. In leadership laboratory, we learned how to be an Air Force officer and were given hands-on leadership training. We were grouped into small flights and alternated being leaders in flight activities when we became juniors and seniors.

The summer between sophomore and junior year, I had to go to boot camp at Westover Air Reserve Base in Massachusetts. It was tough both physically and mentally. We were awakened at 5:00 a.m. every morning, we ran everywhere, and pushed our bodies to the limit the entire time. We were given exactly eight minutes to eat each meal. If we had to change clothes, we were expected to run into the dorms, change, and be back in formation within two minutes. Essentially, boot camp meant that, for four weeks, nothing we did was right, and people were always yelling at us. Boot camp was designed to stress us, break us down, take away our individualism, and build us back up as a member of a team. People told me it would be like that. My mom had been through it herself. She encouraged me ahead of time that it would last only four weeks and that I could get through it. She also assured me that it wasn't the way of all military life. Basically, boot camp was an initiation. It was a once-in-a-lifetime experience, which I was happy to learn later was true. I pushed through, thinking about the end and looking toward the future. I wanted to channel my energy positively, and I threw myself into the physical demands. I survived boot camp using the wisdom and perspective my mom had given me. Without it, I doubt I would have made it, let alone excelled enough to look forward to the next phase of my career.

College was yet another place for me to search for God. I used to walk around the beautiful Villanova campus daydreaming about what God wanted me to do with my life, what his plans were for me, and how I could contribute to a world that was ever expanding before me. I felt like I had skills and talents to put to use, along with abilities, energy, and determination. My friends and I joked that we were all "high on life" and never needed alcohol to stimulate our senses. I felt alive and on fire for God and for helping the world. So, I searched for outlets, wanting to give myself to God. I made friends with all kinds of wonderful people.

My time during college was a natural time of reflection, discovery, and growth. However, also brewing inside were some doubts, which in a few years came to full fruition. These doubts were planted during my senior year of college. Like all students, I was exposed to new and exciting readings in college, which stretched and challenged my mind and imagination. One such book was Marcus Borg's *Meeting Jesus Again for the First Time*. Before I read it, I hadn't been wrestling with doubt. I did wonder about some of the miraculous parts of Jesus' story, like his conception. Now independent and moving toward my future, reading about these questions exposed me to something completely new, thoughts I had never reckoned with before. I had grown up in a life of faith, never questioning the scriptures or my belief in things that suddenly sounded impossible. Maybe everyone must contend with these questions at some point. I suppose they are easier for some to answer than others. My faith was definitely being tested, and it wasn't clear whether it was strong enough to withstand the questions. I see my period of doubt as a spiritual impediment that I was trying to overcome.

At the same time that I was looking for God to cure my doubts, I also experienced the beginnings of a long physical sickness that followed me far beyond college. During the spring of my senior year, I woke up in the small hours of the night feeling like a knife was stabbing me in the back. I thought it was heartburn, though I had never experienced such a searing pain before. I took some Pepto-Bismol and hoped it would clear up. However, that didn't work. After five hours, I went to the school health center and from there was sent to the local hospital for an ultrasound. Everyone suspected gallstones. The usual treatment is surgery, but I wasn't in immediate danger, even after the stones were confirmed by ultrasound. So, I resumed my classes.

Then I started experiencing other strange symptoms. First, a deep, heavy fatigue. I began sleeping for twelve hours a night and still lacked energy. Also, my eyes became extremely sensitive to light. These symptoms were all related to the gallstones. However, I didn't realize it at the time. Somehow, I made it through that final semester of college, despite the pain, exhaustion, and photophobia. I graduated first in my ROTC class and second in my class of math majors. But my gallstone attacks continued and grew worse. I began experiencing short-term memory loss. I had always prided myself on my physical abilities and perseverance and on my sharp memory. Suddenly, all these attributes seemed to be gone.

After graduation, I went to Bethesda Naval Hospital in Maryland to receive treatment and surgery for my gallstone attacks, which came as frequently as every four months. I believed I would have about seven weeks before receiving my first military assignment, enough time to allow for the operation and recovery. Before I could undergo my much-needed surgery, however, my orders came, and I had less than a week to prepare for my first assignment. The surgery would have to wait.

I learned I would be moving to Vandenberg Air Force Base, near Santa Barbara, California, for a year of training.

The drive from Maryland took about three days. Luckily, my dad made the trip with me. We enjoyed the cross-country drive together and completed it straight through. I arrived on the Fourth of July weekend.

Throughout my training year, I continued to need twelve to fourteen hours of sleep each night. I slept even more on weekends. I didn't know that my gallstones were the cause and that leaving it untreated would result in more damage and an inability to do my job. When I went to the doctor on base, I told him that I had a gallstone and that I'd had several gall-bladder attacks. But the doctor didn't order any tests, and I was met with disbelief.

Looking back now, I believe the military doctors had reasons for not listening to me, for not believing my symptoms or that I had gallstones. First, the military has something called the Personnel Reliability Program, which prohibits service members from taking any medications that can interfere with their functions—nothing to make a person drowsy or slow his or her reaction time or alter a person's mental and physical abilities. It's understandable that officers need to be at their best and in top shape to be on missile duty. The dangers and responsibilities of the job are quite real. Yet, the program can cause doctors to turn a blind eye to real health issues, even a crisis, because they are so reluctant to medicate. Second, there's the problem of missile duty itself. The truth is that few people want to be on missile duty. The leadership doesn't treat their people well, and the job is grueling and demanding, the kind that requires living by a checklist. The Air Force was, for these reasons, desperate to get people on missile alert. They were constantly suspicious and simply presumed that anyone with a complaint was trying to get out of missile duty.

The doctor gave me some kind of homeopathic treatment, which did nothing to relieve my pain, and diagnosed me with malnutrition. That went in my medical record—that something was wrong with *me*. That I was not taking care of myself, not eating well, and not being responsible. In addition to exercising and sleeping well, I had always taken great care with my nutrition. I always ate well and had never suffered from an eating disorder. Now I was permanently marked as *malnourished*. The doctor didn't write that down as a side-effect of gallstones but let it stand alone as my diagnosis. I was afraid of what else he might put into my permanent record. I grew mistrustful about whether the military doctors were actually looking out for my best interests, and I quit seeking medical help.

I had a total of nine severe gall-bladder attacks, each one feeling like a knife digging into me. By then I was familiar with the pattern of symptoms. I could predict how long they would last, and I could ride out the pain, fatigue, and light sensitivity. Not only that, everywhere I turned for help, I was met with denial or inattention. My prolonged battle with gallstones caused me an undue amount of stress, both from the physical strains and from not being believed.

The parallels between my spiritual dead-ends and my health crisis were striking. I wanted so badly to give my life to God, yet the doors all seemed closed to my seeking and my spiritual fire. Likewise, I wanted so badly to get well and receive treatment from doctors whom I trusted and relied upon, yet all those doors were closed to me. I felt so alone.

My prayers went unanswered, as did my pleas for medical help. I wondered where God was and where my fellow humans were. I felt forsaken.

Eventually, a few years later, I got the surgery I needed, after much waiting, frustration, and some help from my parents. While I was on leave, my mom arranged for it. She, too, had suffered from a severe gall-bladder issue, and she connected me with her surgeon. It turns out that my father had required the same surgery a few years earlier. I got the help and the relief that I needed, though not through the normal channels. I had to fight and persevere and find my own way. It was yet another parallel to my spiritual journey.

By the end of my training year at Vandenberg, I knew I wanted to pursue orbital analysis, a field that uses mathematics to analyze objects in space. But that was not the path that the Air Force chose for me. I like to say, "Be careful what you wish for." All my life, I wanted God to lead me down his path and put me in his providence, wherever he saw fit. In the end, I got exactly what I wished for: God did lead me, but it turns out that my path and God's path were not always aligned. Many, many times, like this one, my desires were not granted.

Most of my class wanted space jobs. Few wanted to be assigned to missile duty, which had a reputation in the Air Force for treating people poorly. Most of us, however, got assignments as missile operators. There are only three missile bases in the US. I was assigned to Malmstrom Air Force Base in Montana. Despite everything, I was thrilled to be heading to my first job.

My favorite flower

A formal picture of me in the Air Force

A "sign" in New England

My mom and me sitting on the bench outside my house

My mom and dad

My younger brother, Peter

My older brother and his family.
From left to right: Cody, Patrick, Kim, Logan

My nephew, Joey (Peter's son), and his mother, Emily

*My mom, my dad, and me at my graduation
from the University of Notre Dame*

Building a section of the world's largest puzzle

Chapter 5
Malmstrom

*E*ver since I can remember, I have wanted to serve in the Air Force. My mom says that, when I was a small child, I told her that I wanted to work in the Church and be in the Air Force. Those two dreams have never faltered. I have always wanted both.

When it came time for me to begin living my dream of serving in the Air Force, my mom gave me a lot of guidance and wisdom from her career years, for which I am grateful. She had joined the military without anyone there to give her advice, and I often wonder how she made it through. No one told her that boot camp wouldn't last forever, and she came out of that experience thinking her entire military career would involve physical extremes and constant harassment. My mom told me that the Air Force was a system that I had to learn to master. She learned that gaining sponsorship was helpful to getting a good assignment, and she knew there was a process to getting promoted that one had to follow carefully.

My mom also knew that missile duty in the Air Force was an aberration. By this, I mean it was unlike any other component of the Air Force. Missiles was and continues to be a toxic environment. There is a huge gap between top leaders and low-ranking officers. There is little middle management, for lack of a better term, to buffer the two groups or serve as a bridge. The culture was allowed to devolve into something that broke people down, pitted officers against each other, and offered no support or team camaraderie. I heard one story about a missile commander who requested leave to get married. In those days, crew partners were required to take leave at the same time due to a strict policy. The commander's partner refused to take his leave at the same time, so the poor man had to reschedule his wedding.

Recently, Malmstrom was in the news for a cheating scandal that resulted in nine officers being fired. Cheating was happening on officers' monthly proficiency tests. Apparently, many officers were either cheating or knew it was going on. There was so much pressure to perform well, to keep our country safe, to not fail fellow officers or superiors. Unfortunately, it all combined to create a toxic environment that surrounded me during my four and a half years at Malmstrom.

In many ways, my path into the Air Force was set, and all I had to do was follow it. My mom set an example with her own career. Military life was all I knew, and it felt like home. Deep down though, I also missed my childhood in Germany, that idyllic time, my family life, the diversity, the freedom, the acceptance, the military culture, and the core values of integrity, service, duty, honor, and excellence. The

Air Force had provided me with stability and a sense of identity as a child. I knew my job was to aim high, do my best, be honest and respectful, and accomplish a mission. It's no surprise that the Air Force and God felt inseparable to me. Both were about serving a higher purpose, about belonging to something greater than myself. I know now that my Air Force career was in part a search to regain what I had during my childhood: a greater sense of purpose and belonging.

It also became clear to me during my military career that I wanted to continue my studies. I never wanted to stop learning. I still loved math and computer science. I wanted to be on the cutting edge of research, to become a scientist, and join the top-secret Green Door Program (military intelligence). I never received academic mentoring, so I often felt like I missed my chance to continue my studies and go to graduate school. I knew I had the talent, intelligence, and test scores to do well; I just didn't know how to channel everything to fulfill my dream. During my time at Malmstrom, I took correspondence classes to earn a master's degree in computer science. It took me five years to complete the program, all while working full-time.

My duties at Malmstrom included many jobs. I was a squadron scheduler, a deputy missile combat crew commander and instructor, and an assistant flight commander. In addition, I served as a webmaster, technical order officer, safety officer, and squadron command post leader. But it was during my time as a missile combat crew commander that my work began taking a serious toll on my body and mind.

As a missile crew commander, I slept in six-hour shifts: From noon to 6:00 p.m. I would work while my deputy commander slept. Then I would sleep from 6:00 p.m. to midnight, and my deputy would sleep again from midnight to 6:00 a.m. I would take the last shift from 6:00 a.m. to about 10:30 a.m., when the next crew came to relieve us. I worked like this, in twenty-four-hour shifts, barely sleeping.

I worked underground in the Launch Control Center (LCC), a capsule that sits underground and is designed to withstand a nuclear attack. The capsule received 90 percent recycled air and about 10 percent fresh air, and we were sealed inside for twenty-four hours at a time. The LCC's environment was suited to and prepared for war. It had war rations meant to last the crew for a classified number of days. It had a microwave, a small refrigerator, a bathroom, a TV, and just one bed. Since the commander and the deputy rotated sleep shifts, we would just change the sheets each time we used the bed.

The missile work itself was kept tightly to a checklist. I was desperately bored. I had to follow the checklist to the letter, without deviation. There was a set routine, outlined step by step down to the last detail. Imagine cooking with a recipe that said when to get out your cutting board, what kind of cutting board to use, exactly how many slices of onions you needed, or what to do in case one of the slices was a millimeter too thin. Even though missile command was extremely important, it was mind-numbing work. I was young and fresh out of college, full of ambition and energy. I wanted earnestly to use the skills and talents that I was good at to serve my country. My deepest desire was to *design* systems, not just use them. I wanted to be a scientist, to use math and computer science, to follow my passions and do new and interesting work. Instead I was a manager in charge of a checklist.

On top of the monotony and the tedious work, I was surviving on barely any sleep. I hadn't fully recovered from my gallstones and my body's need for increased sleep. But I was getting by on short sleep rotations throughout the day and night. Unlike my mom, who can work just fine on broken-up sleep, I need to sleep straight through the night in order to function. It didn't help that in every spare waking moment I was studying for my master's degree.

At Malmstrom, I had little time to spend on my spiritual life, but I couldn't help but try. I went to Mass on Saturday nights at the base church. To my delight, I found God there again. The chapel at Malmstrom reminded me of the one from my childhood. It was simple, small, and shared by all denominations. I became a lector. The church served the needs of people on base, but it wasn't an active or growing parish. Though it was starting to dim, I still had something of a fire to serve God. I stayed busy like I always did and looked for more places to direct my intense longing to serve. Looking for something new, something outside of my routine, I was disappointed to learn that all the ministries available on base were ones that I had previously been involved with. I already had done choir, altar service, and all kinds of community service. I thought there must be another way for me to use my talents. I was happy to serve in soup kitchens, but I didn't believe that was putting my skills to use. After a few years of finding no outlet, I started dying inside. I was bored at work and with God.

There was nothing new or exciting to grab my attention or catch my spark.

Eventually, my erratic sleep schedule as a missile combat crew commander caught up with me. I was barely functioning, barely surviving. My degree of sleep deprivation was extreme. I was getting two or three hours a night, if I was lucky. My body and mind suffered and nearly shut down. I started getting depressed. A person can take only so much fatigue, stress, frustration, and loneliness.

Near the end of my three-year mark at Malmstrom, I applied to the Air Force Institute of Technology (AFIT). I wanted very badly to be a top-secret scientist in defense of the nation. For reasons that I still don't understand, my commanding officer would not grant me the release I needed to go to AFIT. At some point, I became numb; I couldn't feel anything anymore. Giving my all to the job was constantly met with stress, defeat, or neglect. I could never pursue my passion. I was always told "no." There was no support, the conditions were unhealthy, and nothing was ever going to change. I imagine it was like the feeling one has in an abusive relationship.

Something called a Code 55 kept me from transferring out of my unhappy conditions. The Code 55 says that once a person is assigned to missiles, he or she must stay in that post for four years after training. Part of the reason they do this is the high turnover rate they would have without a mandatory commitment. There was no way out. I had to put in my time.

Toward the end of my tour in missile, in a moment that was rather out of character for me, I reached a very low point. On the phone with my career advisor from inside the capsule, I found myself yelling, "You let me rot in here for five years!" Then I hung up in exasperation. My explosion was the culmination of years of anger, frustration, and depression.

On August 1, 2005, my assignment at Malmstrom finally ended, after five long, exhausting years. I reached the end of my Code 55 and was due to receive my next assignment. My next tour put me in the Civilian Institution Program, which allowed me to go to school full time. I had nearly completed my master's degree, and now I was on my way to a PhD program. All this time, I knew I wanted to be back at a Catholic institution, so I chose and was accepted at the University of Notre Dame for a doctorate in computer science. My future seemed bright. I had sacrificed my physical health and put my dreams on hold for my job, but now I would be able to throw myself into my studies and use my intellect surrounded by others just as passionate about learning as I was.

Looking back, I see now that the Air Force misused its resources in me. I wasn't given the opportunity to live up to my full potential or use all of my skills. At the time they were giving out $40,000 bonuses to keep scientists in the Air Force, but they refused to allow me to use my math and science training and education. Instead they simply used me to fill a position that required minimal technical skill, despite my motivation and eagerness to put myself to better use. And when you don't use math and science knowledge, it fades quickly.

My entire experience at Malmstrom took an enormous toll on my body, mind, and spirit. Maybe I already had a genetic predisposition to mental illness within me. However, I can't help but trace my difficulties to those particular years, where my exhaustion and isolation compounded day after day. I should have been filled with hope and anticipation at leaving Malmstrom for South Bend and a fulfilling educational experience at Notre Dame. But my five years of darkness and strain would not be so easily left behind or forgotten.

Chapter 6
Terminations

*W*hat I remember most about my last days at Malmstrom was the exhaustion. My time there had broken my body and spirit. I was a different person by the end of that tour, no longer the energetic, lively, God-filled achiever I once was. When I wasn't working, all I could do was sleep, but I could never find real rest or begin to heal the deep damage of those months of missile command duty. I was running on empty and had no idea that this would not be the end of my struggles.

The master's degree I had been working on during every spare minute nearly fell apart. My physical and mental state prevented me from finishing my final class. I was forced to ask the instructor for a grade of Incomplete, something I had never done before. I had always seen my commitments through and excelled academically. Finally, the impact of my exhaustion was beginning to show. I was petrified of failing the class and not completing my degree. Eventually, it took me an entire year to finish that last class.

In the meantime, I had two weeks to leave Montana and begin the new phase of my life. I had chosen to pursue a PhD in computer science at Notre Dame because I wanted to be at a Catholic institution. Attending Mass at the little base church at Malmstrom offered a glimmer of hope for my relationship with God. Maybe I would find him again in a new place.

My parents flew out to help me pack and prepare for the twenty-four-hour drive to South Bend. I had two weeks to find a new place to live, and get ready for the start of classes. I was so used to pressing forward and getting things done that I knew of no other way to function. But I was barely hanging on.

The transition from nuclear missile commander to PhD student was harder than I imagined. It should have been a time of great fulfillment, having made it to school at long last. Finally, I would be able to study and learn and exercise my mind the way I desperately wanted to do while I was stuck on missile duty at Malmstrom. I was hopeful about fulfilling my dream to work on the leading edge of technology, to finally be able to design and build the systems that could keep our country safe. My future should have felt bright and full of potential.

But the reality was quite different. Every moment I wasn't in classes or finding my way around a new city, I was working to finish my final master's degree course and erase the Incomplete on my transcript. I was still plagued with anxiety about failing to complete my degree. On top of that, I was enrolled in a year-long training program for officers called Squadron Officers' School. I had to complete this distance course within a short time frame. My life suddenly began to take on an all-too-familiar rhythm: get up, go to school, come home, work, and barely sleep. Every day looked like this—the same kind of grueling, unforgiving routine that I had endured for the past five years. The only difference was that missile duty had been replaced by graduate coursework.

Fourteen months of erratic sleep and utter exhaustion couldn't be undone with a new schedule like this. Nor could I make the mental shift needed to adjust from military life to graduate school. I couldn't get my body back onto a normal sleep schedule no matter how hard I tried. It never occurred to me to take sleeping aids or to see a doctor. During my years in missile command, I was forbidden to take any kind of medication that would interfere with my performance, and I was deeply mistrustful of doctors after my extended battle to receive treatment for my gallstones. I was locked into a mentality that prevented me from getting help and taking steps to fix what was wrong. Leaving Malmstrom should have allowed me to rest and recover, but I was actually setting myself up for worse damage.

Most of the students in my doctoral program were twenty-three years old and right out of college or a master's program. Many were from other countries. Few of them had any real-world work experience, and I felt we had little in common. Additionally, they could not make a decision without what I call "analysis paralysis." Like well-trained graduate students, they had to analyze every detail. This was very different from being a nuclear missile commander trained to make timely decisions. Nor did I have time for friends. The PhD program was an intense three-to-five-year process. It was like a full-time job and much more difficult than the undergraduate experience. Graduate classes are like undergraduate classes on steroids. I was prepared for the level of academic rigor but not for my inability to overcome my exhaustion.

My area of study was computer science. A typical PhD path looks like this: For the first two years, you take classes to become an expert in the field. Then you take qualifying exams that test your advanced knowledge in your subject area. Once you pass your exams, you have to switch gears and devote the rest of your time to doing research and completing your dissertation. The first research component is creating a proposal, which is a one-hundred-page outline of what you will accomplish with your research. It doesn't have to be a step-by-step recipe, because research inherently takes unexpected twists and turns. Then you defend your proposal in front of a committee of professors. Once your proposal is passed and approved, you have the next two years to execute your research plan, write up the results, and try to publish your work in a peer-reviewed scientific journal. Eventually, all your work and results are used to create your dissertation, a book-length project that describes your research, analysis, results, and future work. Once complete, you have to defend your dissertation in front of another committee of professors who grill you with questions and ask you to explain your scientific processes. In the end, they decide whether you pass or fail.

The focus of my dissertation was developing training software for emergency managers. In short, I was designing and developing a distributed, web-based virtual emergency operations center. An emergency operations center (EOC) is a secure location where upper-level emergency officials gather to prepare for, manage, and coordinate the response to an incident (e.g., tsunami, earthquake, hurricane, pandemic). Emergency managers are closely tied to first responders, but they are not the same. First responders are on the scene of an incident and take command of the immediate threat. Typically, they include firefighters, emergency medical technicians, and police officers, either volunteers or paid. Emergency managers, on the other hand, are full-time staff who are removed from the immediate incident and operate at the managerial level to coordinate the response. Their role is not to contain the immediate incident but rather to coordinate resources for the first responders and to manage public relations. It was fascinating and important work that I had waited a long time to begin.

I was already beginning to experience depression in my first year at Notre Dame. I was lonely, stressed, overworked, and just trying to get through each day. I was running into problems with my advisor, who couldn't understand what the last five years had been like for me. What I was experiencing wasn't unlike PTSD. I was experiencing suicidal thoughts. I was consumed by depression and eventually couldn't get out of bed. I wasn't happy, to say the least. I was not my normal self. I didn't know where my normal self had been for a long time. It was impossible for me to find pleasure in anything. Now I know that I was suffering from chemical imbalances, but at the time, I had no idea what was happening to me. I went from working all the time and getting almost no sleep to spending all my time in bed. I was sleeping ten to twelve hours a night. Sometimes, over the course of one weekend, I would sleep for up to forty hours.

I should have sought help, but the idea never crossed my mind. Perhaps I even should have considered taking a break from school to deal with my mental and physical health and try to recover. But taking any kind of break from school would have felt like quitting, and that's not in my makeup. In my family, we just keep working and get through it. Moreover, I had dreamed about school for so long. During all those seemingly endless nights on missile duty, all I ever wanted was to be a scientist, to be intellectually challenged and stimulated. I couldn't give up on that dream during my first year. Had I sought help earlier, my disorder might not have progressed the way it did, and I might not have been sick for quite so long.

For a while, I prayed hard that God would help me. But nothing changed, and I grew angry at God. None of my prayers ever brought me relief. I quit going to church. I lost my faith entirely and felt abandoned and alone. At my lowest, most alienated point, I would have described myself as an atheist.

~

I didn't have any expectations of MIT or Cambridge, Massachusetts. The summer after my first year of PhD study, I received an internship with the Lean Aerospace Initiative (LAI), which had several Air Force ties. I thought the experience would put me on a path to work in research at Hamscom Air Force Base in Boston when I was finished at Notre Dame. It was still my dream to be on the forefront of technological advances and contribute to the defense of our country.

My apartment was in Lowell, MA, about forty-five minutes outside of Cambridge. I drove out alone from Indiana and spent my entire savings on two months of rent. Compared to my house in South Bend, which cost $750 per month, my tiny one-bedroom apartment in Cambridge cost $1,800 per month and nearly wiped me out. Less than a month after arriving, I experienced my first psychotic break with paranoid delusions and my first hospitalization.

Somehow, I got through the rest of the summer and the next fall back in South Bend. I spent the holiday at my parents' home in Waldorf in the winter of 2006. I was still experiencing major symptoms from my psychotic break. After my hospitalization in Boston, I hid my mental illness from Notre Dame. I never told my professors or peers what had happened at MIT. It was my mom who recommended the secrecy, since she knew what kind of damage it could do to my reputation and my career. My mom also put me in touch with a psychologist and a psychiatrist—the same ones who had treated my younger brother, Peter. We thought seeking treatment in Maryland would protect me from having to disclose my diagnosis. We all thought that within a year I would return to normal.

Less than six months after my first break, while home with my parents for Christmas, I got so depressed that I swallowed a bottle of pills my psychiatrist had prescribed. The medications weren't working. I was still lonely, depressed, and delusional, and now I was desperate for some relief, having lost all hope. There were maybe twenty-five pills left in the bottle, and I ingested them right before I got in the car to drive to my therapy appointment.

I blacked out while trying to take a turn too fast and drove straight into a utility pole. By some miracle, no one else was injured, and I walked away from my totaled car without any serious injuries. The police came and helped free me from the wreck. They kept asking what medication I was on, perhaps because my behavior was erratic. They called my parents, who came down to pick me up and take me home.

Perhaps it should have been a clear warning that something needed to change—that I needed to get more help. I don't know if I really wanted to die or if I just wanted to make my suffering go away and didn't know how else to do it. But I pressed on, like I always had. I hid my illness from everyone at Notre Dame and tried to resume my studies.

Needless to say, I didn't do very well when I returned to school. My grades began to slip. I wasn't performing up to standards, and my advisor, who knew nothing about my mental illness, thought I was simply a poor student. When I wasn't in class, I was sleeping to cope with the exhaustion and depression. During classes, I couldn't focus or think clearly. My delusions were intensifying. I thought some of the international students in my program were spies, and I was terrified they would either kill me or capture me as a prisoner of war. I believed they were already hacking into my computer to spy on me, and that I possessed top-secret knowledge that they would torture me to obtain.

I began seeing therapists in South Bend and taking some new medications, but my symptoms were still extreme. I thought the government was out to punish me for every sin I had committed. Every incident from my past, every lie or mean word from childhood, it all came flooding back to me. I believed these were all reasons why the government was persecuting me. I was being made to pay for my sins, no matter how minor or how long ago. Every mistake I had ever made in the Air Force or with my family was exaggerated in my mind. I believed my sins were crimes for which I would be jailed. The government conspiracy was constantly at the forefront of all my thoughts and fears, especially by what I perceived as hypnosis through the radio. I believed my parents were also after me and wanted to punish me. Sometimes even when you're deeply inside a delusion, you can still have a seemingly rational response. I was enraged and incredulous that everyone was coming after me—that as an adult I was being persecuted for my childhood sins. The thoughts wouldn't stop. My medications weren't working.

I continued to keep my mental illness a secret from Notre Dame, but in June 2006, the Air Force discovered that I had been hospitalized for a psychotic break. Proceedings to terminate me from the Air Force began. On March 19, 2007, I was formally discharged. My military career came to an abrupt end. Luckily, I received a full medical retirement with benefits that would help me continue receiving treatment and stay in school.

In my third year of study at Notre Dame, I began work on a grant from the National Science Foundation. My task to design and develop training software for emergency managers fit well with my military experience. At the end of my fourth year, I passed my proposal and secured an internship in Miami to conduct nine months of field research.

I went to work in the Miami-Dade County Office of Emergency Management, specifically with the Geographic Information Systems (GIS) section. As much as I could, I enjoyed my work there. I got to help set up the crisis information management system that they would use to help manage disasters. There were other bright spots in my time there as well. I joined a singles' club called Events and Adventures and participated in lots of activities. I toured the Florida Everglades, where I held a baby alligator, and flew a small airplane for several minutes. I also took a huge road trip with my Aunt Janelle, driving from Miami all the way to Seattle and back. We stayed at various military bases along the way, which offered discounted rates for retirees.

Despite all the good moments, my mental illness retained its hold on me. While in Miami, I ended up in the hospital again. My dad, who had just retired, flew down to be with me.

Eventually, the depression and paranoia grew so extreme, and I was being hospitalized so frequently, that I was forced to tell my advisor about my illness. Back in South Bend after one hospitalization, the university informed me that I needed to meet with the Office of Student Affairs. In the meeting, I was shown a rule from the student handbook that said, if I was a danger to myself, I could be kicked out of school. They said I had to withdraw from my program or I would be withdrawn involuntarily. Utterly devastated, I refused to withdraw. It felt like such a stab in the back, a complete abandonment during my time of greatest need. Yes, I had struggled and hit a low point, but I had never threatened anyone or disrupted the program. I had, in a moment of extreme pain and desperation, cried out for help. Now I was being forced out of school for it. In 2010, I was involuntarily withdrawn from my PhD program for being suicidal.

I deteriorated rapidly from there. Having been removed from my support system and stripped of the work I felt passionately about, I had to leave South Bend and move in with my parents. Because I was no longer a full-time student, my student loans came due. I didn't have a job, nor was I in any shape to start working to repay my loans. The only reason I was able to survive was due to my military retirement and medical benefits.

I thought leaving Malmstrom meant the end of my worst struggles and darkest period. However, I still had a long, difficult road ahead of me.

Chapter 7
Twenty-six
Hospitalizations

*T*he year that my parents and I had predicted it would take to get a handle on my mental illness turned out to be much longer, and it was a much more difficult journey than anyone expected. Between 2006, when I had my first break at MIT, and 2013, I suffered psychotic breaks and hospitalizations in numerous cities, including Baltimore, Washington, DC, Chicago, and across Indiana and Maryland. The incidents varied in their degree of intensity, length of hospital stay, and measure of success in helping me battle my mental illness. No one told me about my diagnosis of schizoaffective disorder. When a person has a psychotic break, he or she is first diagnosed with schizophreniform, while doctors wait to see if the symptoms will disappear. If they last longer than six months, the diagnosis changes to schizoaffective disorder. I didn't learn about all this until I saw the words printed in my military records. In truth, I'm not sure I would have understood the diagnosis anyway. It took years for me to even come to terms with the fact that my mental illness wasn't going away, and that it was, in fact, growing progressively worse each year.

After being forced out of Notre Dame, I lived at home with my parents but tried desperately to hang on to my studies, which I had worked so hard on and which meant so much to me. For a while, my advisor helped me by setting up remote meetings to collaborate on research. We would check in once a week, and I continued making plans to return to school. Thanks to his support, I was eventually readmitted and able to complete my PhD. Nonetheless, it was a long and winding road to the end.

After each hospitalization, I would go on a medication regimen and see a psychiatrist. The antipsychotics and antidepressants didn't seem to be helping. I was very ill and didn't fully understand what was happening. When I took the medications, I experienced debilitating side effects. They caused extreme fatigue, mental fogginess, weight gain, and memory loss. While on the medications, I felt awful, barely able to function. I couldn't understand how feeling like that was supposed to make me better. I had no idea how long it took for the body to adjust to medications and for a person's system to become chemically balanced again. Because I hated the side effects, I would reduce my dosage or stop taking my medicine altogether. It was not in my best interest, and I shouldn't have done it, but I was lost, angry, bitter, and desperate to feel normal again. When I went off my medications, I grew paranoid and delusional. I would experience a break and go into the hospital. I would be prescribed medication, hate the side effects, and stop taking it again. It was a vicious cycle.

Every psychotic break was different. Sometimes I would be taken to the emergency room, then transferred to a psychiatric hospital. Sometimes my parents would have me admitted to the hospital. I was constantly paranoid, believing the television was sending me messages, and that emails were coded with messages from the government. When I walked past a fence, I was thrown into a delusion that I was inside a concentration camp.

Hyper-religiosity was a constant theme in my delusions. Back in 2006, I'd had dreams of becoming an associate with a religious order that I admired. I loved their charism and community service focus. In fact, on my drive from Montana to Indiana, I stayed in several of the order's houses. I was proud and happy to be associated with them, but as my mental illness intensified, our relationship took a turn. I don't know what they believed about me while I was actively delusional, but they stopped all contact and refused to let me become an associate, as planned. I was angry and hurt. I felt abandoned by them and by God. They responded to my attempts at contact with a ban on all communications for nine months.

Unable to work, I turned my attention to regaining my spot at Notre Dame. I was deeply angry after being kicked out of my program. I went online and found a contact form that would send a message straight to the president of the University, Fr. John Jenkins. I just wanted him to hear my story, to listen to what had happened to me. My mom had told me to wait it out—to reapply in a year. I thought it was unfair that I had to reapply to a program I had already been in, and I wanted Fr. Jenkins to know that.

None of my queries to Fr. Jenkins were answered, so I began emailing him directly. I sent emails to him every day. When Fr. Jenkins publicly accepted a generous donation to the school during a televised Notre Dame football game, I saw him smiling at the camera and believed he was talking to me through the screen. I continued emailing him daily.

In 2012, I watched President Obama give the commencement speech at the Air Force Academy. I saw him smiling and talking to the troops and thought he was communicating with me about the military. In 2013, when Jorge Mario Bergoglio was elected Pope and took on the name Pope Francis, I thought it was another sign of communication with me. St. Francis of Assisi was a very meaningful religious figure in my life, and I held his prayer close to my heart. I believed Pope Francis was telling me something when he chose his name, and everything seemed to converge in my mind.

At about the same time, my religious fervor grew and intensified. I felt like my mind was moving at lightning speed, devouring the world's problems and coming up with incredible solutions. It was a period of heightened creativity for me, when I couldn't stop thinking about God or the Church or spiritual dilemmas, for which I invented answers. To the problem of evil and the question of how God could be all loving, all knowing, and all powerful, I came up with an idea about why evil could take hold of the world. I was convinced that I had solved one of the Church's greatest and oldest mysteries.

~

My last psychotic break and hospitalization happened in 2013. I had returned to South Bend, alone, completely detached from reality and unaware of my surroundings. As I walked around town, I saw every fence as part of a concentration camp. My brain told me that we had lost WWII and that the United States was filled with Japanese concentration camps. I drove by a fence and was convinced that I was inside one of those camps. I remembered the code of conduct from my military training, which stated that, if captured by the enemy, I was obligated to give my name, rank, service number, and date of birth. As I turned over my Medicare card and read my social security number, the letter A that followed my number convinced me that I was in "A" camp as a prisoner of war.

I continued wandering the streets, paranoid and afraid of everything. My brain was torturing me. I believed I had been dropped off in the middle of nowhere as part of a military training exercise, and that my duty was to find my way out with no money or supplies in order to prove myself as a military general.

I ended up at a Pizza Hut, begging the employees to call my parents. When they refused, I asked them to call the police. When the officers arrived, I told them I was a prisoner of war and that I needed to find my way out of Texas and get back to my troops. They called an ambulance, and I was taken to the emergency room. I woke up in the hospital still convinced I was inside a concentration camp.

I was transferred from South Bend to a VA hospital in Marion, Indiana, where I was in short-term psychiatric care for three weeks. I spent my days with other psychiatric patients, who I believed were trying to kill me. I thought a serial killer was hiding in our ward, waiting to strangle me. I thought my parents were top-of-the line human-replacement robots. The television was on constantly in the day room where I spent most of the long hours of my stay. The screen mostly blared game shows like *The Price is Right*, but when the news came on, and I heard stories of chemical weapons attacks in Syria, my mind raced with fear that they were aimed at me.

After three weeks in short-term care, I was transferred to the upstairs ward of the VA hospital for ten weeks of long-term care. It was the longest I had ever stayed in a hospital. I was given new medications, and the staff made sure I took them every day. It can take up to five weeks for antipsychotic medication to take effect, for the brain's chemistry to begin to stabilize and respond fully to the medicines. Slowly, my mind cleared. I went from not knowing the date or the name of the president to becoming aware of the reality of my surroundings.

It was the beginning of my truly coming to terms with having a mental illness and accepting it would be part of my life forever. I wasn't going to be cured like my mom or like everyone expected me to be. I have a chronic illness that requires ongoing treatment. I have to see a psychiatrist and take medication to manage my condition. It took a long-term hospitalization with intensive medication and therapy to set me on the path to recovery.

I have not experienced a psychotic break since 2013, nor have I been admitted to the hospital since then. I know I've been lucky to experience the recovery that I have, and

I don't take it for granted. I don't kid myself that another break won't happen. I know it's always a possibility, and I've come close to the edge several times since. It took nearly two years after Marion for my depression to lift. Staying healthy and taking care of myself is my priority now. I have gained the ability to recognize my own symptoms and the signs of my illness. When that happens, I talk to my therapist and my psychiatrist right away and get immediate help.

The brain is a truly remarkable and frightening thing. It can make you see things that aren't real and believe things that never happened. The brain can make the entire world feel like it's converging on your innermost thoughts and secrets. It also can heal from those delusions and form new pathways. But psychosis and delusions are their own kinds of pathways, and once your brain finds a way to make those kinds of neural connections, it's more likely that it will travel down them again in the future. I am constantly vigilant about my mental health.

Throughout everything, the two constants in my life have been my parents and God. Their presence, support, love, and commitment to me have been my rock, my home, and my stability. I have them, along with my doctors and support groups. Now I'm constantly growing and learning and evolving in my relationship with God, my quest to fulfill my vocation, and my journey to maintain my health. My journey is far from over.

Chapter 8
Fighting Irish

I came close to being hospitalized after my stay at the VA in Marion, Indiana. It happened while I was working on a two-month program that was run with such hostility and criticism that my stress level spiked and triggered my paranoia and delusions. Since 2013, however, I have not been hospitalized again. Now I can recognize my triggers and symptoms. The biggest one is stress, which causes my coping skills to go out the window.

It's hard to describe what the onset of a delusion feels like. Often, my mind starts to race. My thoughts come faster and faster, and I can't keep up with my brain. It starts when my brain feels overfilled, burning up with extra energy, moving at lightning speed. There's a sense of hyperactivity and extremely high energy. The other sign is when my brain goes off on tangents and when those tangents start connecting. For example, if I see objects taking on a life of their own, thinking they are trying to send me messages, this is a big tip-off that I need to call my doctors. The blinking lights on a Christmas tree can become more than just lights, like they're part of a government conspiracy. Or it can seem like someone reporting the news on television is trying to get a message to me. Or the Christmas present from my mom is really a package from the military. From there, everything feeds into the same narrative. Random and ordinary things that aren't at all dangerous or suspicious and aren't normally associated with each other start becoming connected in my brain. Everything begins to reinforce a single story no matter how unrealistic or impossible, and everything around me becomes a sign that confirms my delusion. This is when the paranoia sets in and when I start to feel afraid.

During my years of psychotic breaks and hospitalizations, this is what it felt like inside my head. I believed all the connections were real, and I reacted to them as if they were. I was trapped inside my head, seeing and hearing things no one else could, completely alone with these overwhelming fears. The difference today is that I can recognize all these symptoms, and when I do, I don't hesitate to call my doctors. I have managed to stay healthy and address my illness with the help of many forms of support.

I have a psychiatrist whom I see once a month. He monitors my medications and my body's responses to the dosages. He makes sure I stay balanced chemically. He checks to make sure I am cognizant and aware. If I call and say I'm experiencing any of the above symptoms, he gives me permission to increase my dosage of antipsychotic medicine. This is usually enough to bring my brain chemistry back into balance and relieve my symptoms before they turn into a full-blown delusion. Within a few days, I am usually better, and the symptoms go away.

I also have a good psychologist whom I see every two weeks for therapy and check-ins. She monitors me to ensure that I'm keeping myself well and managing my symptoms and the different areas of potential stress in my life. I have known her for years, and I enjoy talking with her, and sometimes we even do puzzles together.

When I lived with my parents in Maryland, I wasn't able to find good doctors to treat me. Today the mental-health community is better, more accessible, and offers more stable support than it did back then. In Maryland, I was assigned by default to the VA hospital and doctors. They were available only for monthly appointments and nothing more. I couldn't call them if I was experiencing a crisis or onset of symptoms outside of my appointment time. I could see them for help one hour a month, and that was it. My doctors in South Bend, on the other hand, are available whenever I need them.

Another difference is that today I manage my energy. What that means is I monitor myself carefully and stay committed to balance. I used to get hit with huge waves of energy, then ride it until I crashed and needed to sleep for twenty hours. Now I maintain control of my energy and try to keep it more consistent. For one, I address my sleep proactively, and I'm committed to taking my medication. If I can't sleep, I take sleep aids, so I'm not up all night, growing exhausted from my brain's overactivity. And I take all my medications regularly. In the past, I didn't listen to my body's need for rest. I would work until I fell over, pushing myself past the brink of exhaustion for missile duty or classes, and then I would crash. Today I make sure that

KATHY ANDERSON

I work only for a specific amount of time, during limited hours in the day, so I have time to rest my mind and body, especially at night. I don't overload myself anymore either. I build in time to care for myself, get enough sleep, and eat well. This is quite different from how I used to live in the military and in graduate school, always running from one demand to the next, taxing and overextending myself, overloading my schedule and having too many things to worry about and take care of.

Each year, I get better. Though I have had periods of discouragement, they are growing less frequent. They are nothing like my hospitalizations. Even among the many different hospitals where I was treated for psychiatric problems, most of those experiences had a lot of similarities. First, I would be taken into the emergency room and evaluated by two doctors to determine if I needed to be treated in a psychiatric hospital. Once in the emergency room, I was not allowed to leave. Sometimes I would wait between twenty-four and forty-eight hours until they found a hospital with an opening to take me.

Right before one of my hospitalizations, I was so desperate to find a lawyer to help me get out that I ripped the phone off the wall in the emergency room. Every hospital has a patient advocate who is supposed to fight for patients. In my experience, they always sided with the hospital, so I never understood the point of having them.

Once in a psychiatric hospital, I was usually strip-searched to make sure I wasn't carrying any weapons. Sometimes, if I was agitated, they would strap me to a bed for hours. I was not given a comfortable bed with a television and nice nurses like you see in movies. Instead, I was locked in small rooms that were arranged so I would not be able to hurt myself. That meant a hard bed nailed to the floor with nothing else in the room. No television to pass the long days, nothing to do but sit there and stare at the walls. If I tried to leave my room, the staff would call a guard to force me back inside. Psychiatric hospitals are extremely cramped. When not in isolation, I usually had a roommate. The bedrooms were often connected to a shared open space, called the day room. That's where we sat and watched television and took our meals. Sometimes I wondered if the government ever inspected those hospitals, and if they had standards for decent facilities and a requirement to offer a humane amount of living space.

What did I do all day long? Mostly, I paced the halls. I paced so much that my feet hurt, but when I asked for medicine to help with the pain, they wouldn't give any to me. Sometimes I attended group therapy sessions that tried to help us focus on basic living skills. One hospital had art therapy, but every day it was always the same activity: making a collage out of pictures cut from old magazines. I might have liked that activity, except all we had were fashion magazines, nothing with nature or science or computers, which would have interested me. Sometimes all I got was a page to color.

Usually, I was given one or two fifteen-minute phone calls a day (only local calls, of course). Several times my parents brought me a jigsaw puzzle or two to work on, because they knew I loved building puzzles. I couldn't complete them, however, because the day room also served as the dining room, and all our tables were cleared off several times a day and used to serve meals. Often the staff would clear the tables during the night and sweep my half-finished puzzle back into the box. Many times, I left the hospital in worse condition than when I went in.

I think about all these experiences today, and I'm grateful and relieved that I have not been back since 2013. But I am also frustrated at the state of our country's mental-health services and the conditions that sick people are forced to experience when they need the most help. I think about how many hospitalizations it took before I could get well and why the process took so long and involved so much difficulty and suffering. I know today that I have a chronic illness that needs to be monitored and treated. I know that someday I may have to go back into a psychiatric hospital if something happens to me. I've come close. The reality of my illness means it's always a possibility.

~

In January 2013, I reapplied to my PhD program at the University of Notre Dame. I was angry that I had to reapply to a program for which I had completed all of my coursework, not to mention that I was already working on my dissertation. It had been two and half years since I had been forced to leave the program. I was determined to complete the curriculum and earn my degree. I also wanted to move back to South Bend and try to work with the psychiatrist who had given me his support and recommended that I be allowed to re-enter the PhD program.

After another fourteen months, I was readmitted and got back to working with my previous advisor. During my time in Maryland, he had kept up communication with me and encouraged me to keep writing my dissertation. When funding allowed, he even tried to continue collaborating with me on research. Now that I was back in the program, I needed to complete one final semester of work. I also needed to finish writing my dissertation, create a presentation of my research, and defend it in front of my committee. I am proud to say that I completed all of these tasks and earned my doctorate in computer science. Not only that, a few years later, I finished my second master's degree in applied mathematics, also at the University of Notre Dame. My work and the program went much smoother than before. I also learned a great deal about the purposefully difficult way STEM subjects are taught in school.

Never one to cease learning, in 2019 I was accepted into another master's program, this time in data science. I cannot wait to dive into my new field of study and complete another degree. I love challenging myself and furthering my education, and my window of opportunity to use the GI Bill expires in less than two years. Once I retired from the Air Force, I had fifteen years to make use of the GI Bill in whatever way I wanted. I wasted no time going back to school and staying in school to learn as much as I could. I could stop and be satisfied with my degrees and all my education, but I love academics, and how could I just leave all that opportunity on the table? How can I not use what little time I have left to get the most out of my learning opportunities?

My mental-health and educational journeys are far from over. The same is true of my faith journey. Finding my faith again has been a slow, gradual process. It began by reengaging with church activities in South Bend. I found some community-service opportunities and slowly started finding my way to helping others. My faith is still a deep part of me. I certainly felt like an atheist at my lowest points, wondering where God was and why he had abandoned me. I was angry at God, confused about what he was doing with my life, and in despair at what he had let happen to me. Despite everything, I was still thinking about God. I still believed there was someone to be angry with, someone whose absence I could feel.

When I was in college and throughout my most difficult years, I was much more intellectual about my faith. It was something I read about on paper. Faith had not come alive in my heart the way it had when I was a young child, in love with God and sure of his presence in my life. I look at my doubts today not as something that destroys my faith but as a pathway to greater growth and understanding.

This year, a remarkable thing happened to me. On my birthday, which also happens to be the feast day of St. Francis of Assisi, I was invited to join the third order of St. Francis. It's like an answer to my previous disappointment with never becoming an associate with a women's religious order. It's like my faith life has come full circle. I am excited about my new role and this new community I will join. It will include community service, masses, meetings, and a whole new set of opportunities for my faith and my relationship with God. This part of my story is waiting to be written.

~

In August 2015, I was attending a program for the National Science Foundation when I got a call from my mom. She needed me to come home right away. When I got there, I learned that my little brother, Peter, had died. He was only thirty-two years old. He died in his sleep of a heart arrhythmia that caused cardiac arrest. He was doing so well in life, and I was so proud of him.

I had dreams about Peter's death. Never about any of my other family members, only Peter. He lived a good life, and I was proud of him. Peter matured a little later than other kids, right around the age of twenty-seven. He had the opportunity to do some great things in his short life, including living in Europe with our family for the first part of his life, making and keeping many great friends, going to college, writing and publishing three books, getting his dream car—a Dodge Challenger—and having a son, who is now ten years old and living in New Hampshire. I am lucky that I can see him a few times a year. My parents aren't far from him either. Even though Peter is gone, his spirit is still with us. He managed to do a lot in a short amount of time. He is well remembered.

I know now more than ever that life is short and that it is a gift. Just this Thanksgiving, I spent the weekend with Patrick and his family. I had a lovely time, and I can see that relationship finding a new beginning as well. I look back on my period of mental illness differently now, with understanding and forgiveness for the past. I think he does too. We're growing closer gradually. We are overcoming all of the past—learning and moving forward.

It's clear to me today that being off my medicine is dangerous. I will always have to manage my illness and stay vigilant about taking care of myself. It hardly makes sense to me anymore how I got by while I was delusional. When you're inside an active delusion, there's no way to check yourself or find your footing in reality without a great deal of help. When I'm sick, I'm prone to irrational thoughts and poor judgement. My mind gets distorted, and my imagination goes wild. I used to think that, if a person was not harming others, he or she shouldn't be hospitalized. Now I realize it's in someone's best interest to be treated no matter what—that facing mental illness and getting help is the best thing for everyone, including me.

I learned how to persevere throughout my struggles. I learned never to give up. Mental illness does not let up, and neither can I. It's a daily requirement and sometimes a daily struggle. My dad likes to say, "It's so damn daily." He's right. It is. But we are lucky to have the days at all.

Epilogue
Lilies in the Field

*T*oday my life looks like this: I live in South Bend. I fill my days with many different things, but every day I try to do a little ACE: achieve, connect, and enjoy. I do a little something every day to create a sense of achievement, connect with different people, and enjoy an activity. I participate in the crochet ministry and the young-adult ministry at my church. I teach classes at the Forever Learning Institute, helping senior citizens learn to use computers and helping the institute revamp its registration process and database. I also participate in Just Faith, a program about Catholic social teaching. I help others when I can, offering rides and personal help to people in my community.

I'm retired from the military, and I receive full medical insurance and benefits. It allows me to spend my time learning and helping others. I struggled to find my way in life and discover what would truly fit me and help me feel fulfilled. It has been a long, slow process, but I'm beginning to feel at home in South Bend, having lived here on and off for over fourteen years—the longest I've ever been in one place in my entire life. I have a handle on my mental illness. It's never easy, but I know how to cope with depression, dark thoughts, and signs of a relapse.

When I think about the most difficult and dark times of my life—those five years at Malmstrom and all those hospitalizations—I see it all from a different perspective now. My view includes a great deal of gratitude for the life I am able to have right now. With a full military retirement and benefits, I'm able to pursue my many interests—academic, creative, and spiritual.

In the summer of 2017, I went to the New York Film Academy to take a 3D-animation class. I have plans to adapt my brother Peter's stories into short animated films as a tribute to him. I have even more plans to work in mobile application programming and web development. I have my parents and my older brother, as well as extended family, a network of professional support, and my church community.

I've changed a lot over the past decade. I used to keep extremely busy, but I've slowed down, and I like the pace of life today. I don't like having stressful deadlines. I like savoring each day as it comes. I like sitting in silence, reflecting, working on my puzzles, and reading.

Among the many things I've learned are the following bits of wisdom: Don't judge others. There are many factors I can't see in another person's life. Don't burn bridges. I need to keep myself well, so I can help others. Ask open-ended questions, and use "I" statements. Don't try to change people. It's good to express my needs. Most things are temporary. Praise in public, criticize in private. Be proactive to get what I want. Strive constantly to learn more. Life is a tradeoff. Work like it depends on you, and pray like it depends on God. There is a path forward; don't backpedal. Get your education. Don't hold a grudge. Anger mostly happens because of a difference in expectations. My experiences are different from others. Life is what you make of it. Comparison is the thief of joy. I can do almost anything.

For the many people in the world who struggle with mental illness, I hope they find peace and help, and I hope they hang in there and know that, despite the dark moments, life contains a great deal of hope and goodness. I find encouragement in the words of St. Therese of Lisieux, who lived by the ideal of "the little way," which means looking for holiness in everyday tasks and the people in our lives. It takes time, but recovery is possible. For me, recovery has meant working twice as hard since medication affects my memory. I know I can still contribute a great deal to society as a volunteer, family member, and friend. So can anyone else, as long as we all keep moving forward and keep trying to see the light.

My greatest lesson from my long journey has been that everyone has a vocation. This includes the mentally ill, perhaps most especially. Delusions of a hyper-religious nature are often dismissed, instead of seen as a way that God manifests himself in all people, how he is continuing to work in their lives and give them vocations. Mental illness, like any disability, does not make you worthless, though it may certainly feel like that sometimes. Every human being has value, especially those struggling with their brain chemistry. I know now that God healed me in his own way and in his own time. He continues to heal me today.

I have kept my desire to do God's work with my life, to bring heaven to Earth, and to build God's kingdom here. Part of my vocation, and that of every person, is our call to be saints in our own lives.

~

I remain open to what God wants to do with my life. I gave my life to God again within the past year. I let go and said I would do whatever God has planned for me. I was hesitant to do that again, since the first time when I left it all up to God my life was turned upside down. Now I know in my heart that God only wants what's best for me. I know God is not punishing me for anything. He's not hurting me. I know I had an illness, and it wasn't anything that God was doing to me.

God continues to move in my life, bringing me opportunities and mysteries that I might not fully understand but that I am grateful for, nonetheless. I find God in the fullest part of my days and in the unscheduled moments of quiet. I find God in my moments of recovery and on the winding path that brought me through my setbacks. I find God in my family and my future. My story has taken unexpected turns through many places and with many people, and all the while, God has been with me. This is how faith works. Faith carries us through the dark and the light and delivers us exactly as God intended—loved and created in his image. He cares for us like he clothes the lilies in the field.

About the Author

Kathy Anderson is a retired Air Force captain who holds a PhD in computer science from the University of Notre Dame. Born in the Netherlands, Kathy lived near Air Force bases in the Netherlands and Germany until age eleven when she, along with her parents and two brothers, moved to Waldorf, Maryland. With her sights set on a military career, she earned a BA in math from Villanova University while enrolled in the ROTC. Her work in missile defense spanned several states and command positions before she earned her master's in computer science from the University of Massachusetts-Amherst, then went into the Civilian Institution Program to earn her doctorate. Today she is retired and living in South Bend, Indiana, where she focuses on software engineering, community service, and building the world's largest jigsaw puzzle. *Lilies in the Field* is her first book.